AF430847

designed + published by c7marketing boutique

visit <u>c7marketing.co/asmp</u> for free tools + resources

Year_________________

COMPANY INFORMATION

Business Name

Business Description

Products/Services

Social Media Handles

COMPANY DESCRIPTION

Mission

____

____

____

____

Vision

____

____

____

____

Values

____

____

____

____

This Year's Goals

____

____

____

____

BRAND

Voice (funny, serious, casual, professional)

____

Personality (excitement, sincerity, ruggedness, competence, and
sophistication)

____

____

Promise (experience customers can expect to receive with every interaction)

____

____

Values (integrity, accountability, diligence, perseverance, discipline, etc.)

____

____

Positioning (product's value proposition placed within the context of the
market landscape)

____

____

____

BRAND IDENTITY

Colors

____

____

Imagery (llustrations, line art, or photos that are detailed, soft focus, zoomed in effect, etc.)

____

____

____

Font

____

____

____

Slogan

____

____

____

____

TARGET AUDIENCE

Customer Avatar

Name   Age
____

Location
____

Family status
____

Personality
____

Core Values

____

____

Activities + Interests

____

____

Customer Pain Points

____

____

How does your product/service solve their problem?

____

____

____

CONTENT

Is there a cause associated with the problem you solve?

____

____

____

Content Themes (3-4 discussion topics aligned with your product/service)

____

____

____

____

Which marketing channel fits you best? (social media, email, in-person, etc.)

____

____

____

____

____

SEO + KEYWORDS

Product/Service

____

Keywords/Phrases

____

____

____

____

Product Description Using Keywords

____

____

____

____

Keywords + Phrases to Avoid

____

____

____

____

COMPETITOR ANALYSIS

Competitor Name

Product + Features

Market Share

Pricing

COMPETITOR ANALYSIS

Differentiators

Strengths

Weaknesses

COMPETITOR ANALYSIS

Marketing

Culture

Customer Reviews

BUSINESS PERFORMANCE

Business Performance	Prior Year Actual	Current Year Actual	Current Year Plan
Revenue			
EBITDA			
Total # Employees			
Revenue/Employee			
Profit/Employee			

Cost of Marketing + Sales
———————————————— = Customer Acquisition Cost $ ________
New Customers Acquired

What is this year's total marketing budget?

____

Where did your best customers come from?

____

____

What improvements can you make to attract your best customers?

____

____

How can you improve your product/service to attract your best customers?

____

____

GOALS

Annual Goals

Q

- [ ]
- [ ]

Q

- [ ]
- [ ]

Q

- [ ]
- [ ]

Q

- [ ]
- [ ]

Q____

QUARTERLY STRATEGY

QUARTER_____BUDGET

Category	Month Spend	Month Spend	Month Spend	Total
Totals				

CONFERENCES

Date	Conference Name	Cost

SPEAKING ENGAGEMENTS

Date	Conference Name	Speaking Fee	Total Cost

BLOG

Date	Keywords	Title

EMAILS

Date	CTA	Message

SOCIAL MEDIA

Date	Platform	Message

SOCIAL MEDIA

Date	Platform	Message

ADVERTISING

Date	Platform	Product/ Service	Message

INFLUENCER

Name   Cost

Contact Information

Message

Name   Cost

Contact Information

Message

STREET MARKETING

Location

____

____

Resources + Strategy

____

____

____

____

Location

____

____

Resources + Strategy

____

____

____

____

WEBINAR

Date + Time

Title

Description

Speakers

Offer

WEBINAR

Date + Time

Title

Description

Speakers

Offer

WEBINAR

Date + Time

Title

Description

Speakers

Offer

WEBSITE

Notes

GOOGLE MY BUSINESS

Notes

____

____

____

____

____

____

____

____

____

____

Notes

____

NOTES

NOTES

NOTES

NOTES

NOTES

Q____

QUARTERLY STRATEGY

QUARTER_____BUDGET

Category	Month Spend	Month Spend	Month Spend	Total
Totals				

CONFERENCES

Date	Conference Name	Cost

SPEAKING ENGAGEMENTS

Date	Conference Name	Speaking Fee	Total Cost

BLOG

Date	Keywords	Title

EMAILS

Date	CTA	Message

SOCIAL MEDIA

Date	Platform	Message

SOCIAL MEDIA

Date	Platform	Message

ADVERTISING

Date	Platform	Product/Service	Message

INFLUENCER

Name   Cost

____

Contact Information

____

____

Message

____

____

____

Name   Cost

____

Contact Information

____

____

Message

____

____

____

STREET MARKETING

Location

____

____

Resources + Strategy

____

____

____

____

Location

____

____

Resources + Strategy

____

____

____

____

WEBINAR

Date + Time

Title

Description

Speakers

Offer

WEBINAR

Date + Time

Title

Description

Speakers

Offer

WEBINAR

Date + Time

Title

Description

Speakers

Offer

WEBSITE

Notes

GOOGLE MY BUSINESS

Notes

NOTES

NOTES

NOTES

NOTES

NOTES

Q____

QUARTERLY STRATEGY

QUARTER_____BUDGET

Category	Month Spend	Month Spend	Month Spend	Total
Totals				

CONFERENCES

Date	Conference Name	Cost

SPEAKING ENGAGEMENTS

Date	Conference Name	Speaking Fee	Total Cost

BLOG

Date	Keywords	Title

EMAILS

Date	CTA	Message

SOCIAL MEDIA

Date	Platform	Message

SOCIAL MEDIA

Date	Platform	Message

ADVERTISING

Date	Platform	Product/Service	Message

INFLUENCER

Name   Cost

Contact Information

Message

Name   Cost

Contact Information

Message

STREET MARKETING

Location

Resources + Strategy

Location

Resources + Strategy

WEBINAR

Date + Time

Title

Description

Speakers

Offer

WEBINAR

Date + Time

Title

Description

Speakers

Offer

WEBINAR

Date + Time

Title

Description

Speakers

Offer

WEBSITE

Notes

GOOGLE MY BUSINESS

Notes

NOTES

NOTES

NOTES

NOTES

NOTES

Q____

QUARTERLY STRATEGY

QUARTER_____BUDGET

Category	Month Spend	Month Spend	Month Spend	Total
Totals				

CONFERENCES

Date	Conference Name	Cost

SPEAKING ENGAGEMENTS

Date	Conference Name	Speaking Fee	Total Cost

BLOG

Date	Keywords	Title

EMAILS

Date	CTA	Message

SOCIAL MEDIA

Date	Platform	Message

SOCIAL MEDIA

Date	Platform	Message

ADVERTISING

Date	Platform	Product/Service	Message

INFLUENCER

Name   Cost

____

Contact Information

____

____

Message

____

____

____

Name   Cost

____

Contact Information

____

____

Message

____

____

____

STREET MARKETING

Location

Resources + Strategy

Location

Resources + Strategy

WEBINAR

Date + Time

Title

Description

Speakers

Offer

WEBINAR

Date + Time

Title

Description

Speakers

Offer

WEBINAR

Date + Time

Title

Description

Speakers

Offer

WEBSITE

Notes

GOOGLE MY BUSINESS

Notes

NOTES

NOTES

NOTES

NOTES

NOTES